Yesteryear
in Smithfield
and Point Marion

by Marci Lynn McGuinness

Published by Shore Publications
P. O. Box 26, Chalk Hill, Pennsylvania 15421

Copyright © November 1996
Second Printing 2008

ISBN: 978-0-938833-13-0

Cover Photo contributed by Gordon C. Baker. This group of men is from left to right standing: Jimmy Costello, Alph Miller, Eck McClain, Grant McClain, George Hasting, Alvic Johnson, and John Crowe (the cook). Seated: Charles Frankenberry, Alph Frankenberry, Noah Johnson, and Isaac (Ike) Blosser.
The photo was taken in McKeesport after this group of Point Marion men hauled a load of logs there on the wooden raft shown.

FORWARD

Dear *Yesteryear* Readers:

I would like to introduce you to my fourth book in the *Yesteryear* series, *Yesteryear in Smithfield & Point Marion A Pictorial History*. This, like the Ohiopyle and Masontown books, is a compilation of photographs which tell the history of the towns visually. They are meant to be a keepsake of memories for those who lived through "the good old days" and an education to younger generations who know little of their past.

In order to create these works, the co-operation of many is required. Because of their generosity in lending me their photographs and their patience as the publication date moved further and further away, I would like to thank the following contributors:

Gordon C. Baker, Jane Liston, Anna Malone, W. Don Jordan, Bill Duffy, James Breakiron, Mrs. John W. Phillians, Mrs. J. W. Weller, The Smithfield Library, Scott Novak, William G. Brown, Dorothy D. Smith, Wayne Reese, Mrs. C. M. Weller, Walter E. Lytle, Bernice Morgan, Mina Porter, Mrs. B. Berchinal, Rose Nestor, Pauline Rosinsky, Albert Seghi, Roy ....., Warren Monaghan, Smithfield Rotary Club, and Mrs. Eleanora D. Williams.

I would also like to thank Keith Franks and all those at Masontown Printing who have worked diligently to help transform all the *Yesterear* books into book form.

The next book in the *Yesteryear* series will be published in the fall of 1996. It is entitled *Yesteryear at the Uniontown Speedway*. This will be a hardbound book covering the famous wooden race track that ran from 1916-1922 in Hopwood, the Summit Mountain Hill Climbs which preceded it, and the dirt track Speedway of the 1940's.

I hope you enjoy *Yesteryear* and that these nostalgic books touch your hearts!

Sincerely,

Marci Lynn McGuinness

Marci Lynn McGuinness
Backwoods Books Publisher

CONTENTS

YESTERYEAR IN SMITHFIELD

THE COOLEY GANG

DOWNTOWN STREETS AND STORES

CHURCHES AND SCHOOLS

THE RAILROAD AND MINES

HOTELS, HOUSES, FARMS

PEOPLE

YESTERYEAR IN POINT MARION

INDUSTRY

THE TOWN

HOTELS AND HOUSES

THE RIVER

CHURCHES AND SCHOOLS

The Cooley Gang - Fayette County Desperados

On September 27, 1892, the Pittsburgh Times referred to them as the "Fayette Desperados" The Cooley Gang of Fairchance was both feared and loved as they robbed the well-to-do and gave to the poor, not unlike Robin Hood himself. But did Robin Hood burn the bottoms of his victim's feet? Not that I have ever read.

The Cooley Gang was made up of five men and a "Queen" They were Brent Frye, Sam Yeager, Frank Cooley, Jack Ramsey, and Jack Cooley. The lady known as "The Queen" was Lida Patterson, who traveled with them at times. Their rein lasted about five years and the stories about their escapades vary greatly.

The gang lived in the mountains across the way from Frank Martin's farm. They existed by robbing milk houses and forcing people to give them the money they had hidden in their homes. Most folks did not use banks at that time. When the gang was being sought by the law, they often hid out in Delaney's Cave (Laurel Caverns) or the Tent Church in Fairchance.

The gang was so popular during the late 1880's and early 1890's that other outlaws copied their style. This caused the men to be blamed for some crimes for which they were not responsible. But they were responsible for many, one of which occurred on the Jacob Prinkey property in Gibbon Glade. According to the Connellsville Courier issued September 30, 1892, the Cooley Gang paid Jacob Prinkey a visit on Saturday night (six nights before this article appeared as news traveled slow at that time). Prinkey was a well-to-do farmer and stock raiser. He also manufactured grain cradles and kept his savings hidden at home. Prinkey considered banks unsafe and inconvenient.

Prinkey told the story to the Courier like this, "Myself and family were sitting paring peaches when we heard a rush of feet on the porch outside. We had been anticipating robbers for some time, and my son, aged 25, had time to grab his revolver from his jacket before five men with masks on them and revolvers in each hand rushed into the room. They came huddled together as close as possible. When they entered my son fired one shot, but before he could fire more the gang was upon him and took his revolver. Two members of the gang kicked and pounded him and finally bound and tied him to a chair. The shot had struck two of the robbers. The first fellow was seriously hurt and was taken outside. The other was slightly cut under the left arm, was a large man, and determined to do my son damage but one of the gang I took for Ramsey wouldn't let him. My wife and granddaughter were almost frightened to death and were screaming at the top of their voices. At this point I contrived to take a hand. I slipped behind the kitchen door and got a Winchester rifle. I cocked the gun to fire but just as I was about to pull the trigger I thought my son might be among the gang and let the gun down. I was presently discovered and the gun taken from me although I tried hard to fight. I was bound and tied to a chair, as were my wife and granddaughter.

When we were all tied they went out to where their wounded lay on the porch. They prepared a milk and bread poultice for him and one of the men took off his hat and put it on the wounded man. I couldn't tell how badly the man was hurt but the wound must have been bad. I can't tell which one of the gang it was but from what I saw and heard I am sure that the one hurt most was Frank Cooley and the other, Yeager. After attending to the wounded, they went through the house and got $20 in money, a lot of clothing, my Winchester rifle, and two revolvers. I think there were seven to the gang as there were five in the house and I think two outside.

We had rather been expecting such an attack as a neighbor's milk house had been robbed and on Saturday morning he had discovered the gang in rendezvous in full view of my house. From appearances they had been there for some time. Strewn about were pieces of playing cards and on some of them were Sam Yeager's name. Sticks about the size of a policeman's were found in the house the next morning. Sunday morning a posse went in search of the gang but could not overtake them. They escaped over the mountain toward Uniontown and Fairchance where the cave they are said to inhabit during the winter months is located."

More examples of the lawless gang were incidents like the winter day in 1888 when they visited Mollie Ross, who was a spinster living at the foot of the mountain near Smithfield. Three rough men entered her home and encouraged her to tell where her money was kept by using kerosene lamps to burn the soles of her feet. The gang came away with a resounding 12 cents.

They once robbed the Beeson Works mine of $2,700.

Charlie Lewis, head of the Lewis gang is said to have been sadistic. Frank Cooley was his apprentice. This is who taught him to burn people's feet. Frank was so good at torture, he formed his own gang and thereby made history. Jack Ramsey of McClellandtown fingered homes for the gang. Out of the five households in the small village where they tortured and robbed, they netted $200 and a few horses. They laid low in a cabin in Markleysburg after those incidents and ventured to Somerset County where they found an old Amishman and proceeded to burn him and hang him from a rafter. It was after this that a posse was formed and the Lewis Gang caught and imprisoned.

Local residents were putting immense pressure on lawmen to capture The Cooley Gang, but no one had the guts to stand up to them.

But finally George Fisher, a United States secret service detective from Hagerstown, MD, Frank Pegg of Uniontown, Policeman Hartley of Fairchance, Sheriff McCormick, and deputies quietly watched the gang for several weeks. They saw that they regularly came down from their mountain hideout on Sundays to "Old Man

Cooley's" to play cards and drink. This Sunday, Frank Cooley and Jack Ramsey rode in about noon. In the afternoon the two men went out in back of the house and were resting against stumps when the Sheriff and his men advanced. After exchanging about five shots with Cooley, the Sheriff moved behind a tree and fired the fatal shot which pierced Cooley's heart while he still lay there against the stump. He died immediately. Ramsey fled while deputies fired but he got away. This happened just one week after they robbed the Prinkey's and evidence of a partly healed bullet wound found on Frank Cooley's body confirms Prinkey's account of that incident. Ramsey was pursued and caught two days later, the last of the gang to be stopped. Frank Cooley's funeral was attended by over 1,000 people. It is said that the breaking of the gang came through Sam Yeager who had been arrested earlier and betrayed his comrades for a promise of a portion of the reward and immunity from punishment. In December of that year The Cooley Gang was sent up the river. Jack Ramsey was sentenced to 19 years in the Penitentiary, seven of which were for his part in the Prinkey robbery. Two other men of the gang, Charley David and William Martin, were sentenced that day to 5 1/2 years each. Yeager was given 18 months in the workhouse as he had turned state's evidence and was wanted in West Virginia on more charges. The "Queen" was given leniency because of her infant child. She was sent to the work house for 18 months and ordered to pay court costs. Harriet Abel Cooley (mother of the outlaws) and two daughters and a younger son were tried and given suspended sentences for receiving stolen goods.

Main Street at the head of Liberty Street - circa 1900.

The foot of Liberty Street at the railroad crossing. Booty Fields pictured, facing the B & O shop.

Liberty Street looking north.

Water Street looking north. The school house would be on the right going uphill.

Church Street. Notice the men on the right in front of Guy Feather's Store and on the left at the old Post Office, passing the time of day.

This is High Street, around 1910-1915

1916 - Building the road from Smithfield to Ruble. On the shovel, left to right are Stanley Smith and Ralph McLaughlin. In front of the shovel, left to right are Jesse Swaney and Percy Coates. Mr. Evans stands to the right of the wagons with his arms folded. The wagons and teams of horses belonged jointly to James Miller of Ruble and the man who owned the land adjoining the road, William "Little Bill" Breakiron. Photo taken at the top of the "S" curve beyond the railroad underpass at the bottom of Water Street, just beyond Georges Creek.

The road from Smithfield to Ruble was built in 1916 by the P. D. Coates Company of Uniontown. On the steam shovel in the back of the photo are Ralph McLaughlin on the left and Stanley Smith on the right. Standing on the left next to the bank, third man to the left is Percy Coates. On the wagon closest to the shovel is Beanie Groover. Bill Lynn is in the third wagon from the back. Standing to the left of the wagon in the front of the photo is Jessie Swaney. Notice the box on the bank in front of the shovel. It has a pipe coming out from below it. The workers put their greasy clothes in this box and ran a pipe from the shovel to the extended pipe, using the steam to clean their clothes. This road was bricked in 1917 and black-topped in 1939.

A. J. Sutton's store on Main Street, decorated for Memorial Day, 1912. From left to right: Clair Costello, Pauline Hall, Mabel Sutton Costello, A. J. Sutton, John Howard, and George Grimm.

Dunn's General Store and Pharmacy on Main Street. From left to right are: S. Dunn, the druggist; Cora Dunn, Sara Dunn, and Guy Feather.

George Grimm's Store around 1920. This is now Nicossia's.

Matthews' Store on Main Street during the late 1920's. Orville Matthews standing to the left.

The Sutton Building Restaurant around 1922. Paul Howell and Charles Miller at counter. This is where today's Smithfield Hardware sits.

1905 at G. A. Feathers. From left to right: Frank Stuck, Orville Howard, Squire O'Neil, Guy Feather (in doorway), James Huhn with cane, the little girl is a Sutton, Abraham, a Strumm in the derby hat, unknown, Beany Groover, Rohrer, Andrew Sutton, William Abraham, Ethel Sutton, Jennie Rankin, John C. Howard on "Prince" (the horse).

The Wharton Supply Company served the coal mine near the Weaver Property from around 1900 through the 1920's. It was owned and operated by J. W. Weaver.

The A. A. Moser Store in Ruble, 1901-1902.

J. C. Doolittle's Store and house around 1900. This is where Reese's Wholesale sits today.

Looking down Liberty Street at the Black Brothers Livery, circa 1900.

The Weaver's Mill after converting to steam around 1915.

The old Post Office on Main Street around 1905. These are believed to be mail buggies. Ethel Sutton Grannell is shown to the right. She worked in the Post Office alongside her father, Andrew J. Sutton, who was Postmaster for 24 years. Mr. Grimm stands to the far left in front of his shop.

The old Smithfield Library.

Old Smithfield Post Office, built in the late 1870's.

The Smithfield State Bank was built in 1925.

Mt. Moriah Baptist Church was built in 1863. This photo was taken during the 1920's.

The Mt. Moriah Baptist Church in background and Wise's Garage in center.

Mt. Moriah Baptist Church Loyal Daughters Class, January 9, 1947 Left to right, seated: unknown, unknown, Teacher Earl Morgan, Kate Morgan, kneeling; Maude Vance, Clara Cooley, and Bell Shoaf. Standing: Dora Brown, Orpha Hague or Maude Morgan?, Nan Shoaf, unknown, unknown, Mary Thomas, Mirah Lowe, Della Jenkins, Clara Morton, unknown, unknown.

Woodbridge Church, circa 1905.

Jennie Moser's Sunday School Class at Woodbridge, 1907. The second boy from the right in front is Lloyd Fowler.

Woodbridge Sunday School Group of 1938. Kneeling, left to right: Freda Means, Erma Van Sickle, Virginia Mae Fowler, Dolores Fowler, Happy Powell, Nellie Grimwood, a Blair, Mamie Farr, Margaret Price, Effie Moser, Doris Lynn, unknown, and unknown. Seated: Martha Feathers, unknown, Betty Dunham, Loretta Fowler, Nellie Dunham, Ruth Price, Ruth Feathers, unknown, Eleanor Price, unknown, and unknown. Third Row: Virginia Anderson, unknown, Lucille Conn, Thelma Powell, Mary Darrell, unknown, unknown, Martha Moser, Mary Price, Charles Price, Bill Brady, Oakie Feathers. Back row: Nellie Fowler, Della Mae Darrell, the next five are unknown, Myrtle Fowler, Emma Feather, Playford Van Sickle, and the man in front between row three is Darrell King.

Mrs. Feather's class of 1938 at Woodbridge Sunday School. Front row, left to right: Martha Feathers, Darrell King, Playford Van Sickle, and Bill Brady. Standing: Dolly Fowler, Myrtle Feathers, Lucille Conn, Catherine Feathers, Thelma Powell, Goldie Fowler King, Martha Moser, Thelma Fowler, Emma Feathers, Virginia Anderson, Ella Mae Della.

The Smithfield 5th and 6th grade class of 1910 - Eleanor Woodfill, teacher.

The Smithfield School Basketball, 1914. Left to right: Walter Morgan, Connie Costlow, Bill Robinson, Chet Conn, and Lawrence Scat Hankins.

Smithfield High School students, 1943. First names are on photo.

Smithfield School, 1939-1940. Front row, left to right are: Velma Cussins, Rosie Sadler, Hilda Cussins, Laura Breakiron. Second row: Bobby Kovach, Jim Van Bremen, Don Jordan, Jim Sandusky, Fred Michotte, Jack Van Bremen, Bill Leech, Lynn McCann, Dick Kovack. Third row: Ocie Sadler, Mary Hotsinpillar, Sue Bowman, Dolores Kennison, Lorraine Leckemby, H. Coughenour, Patty Miller. Fourth row: unknown, Vivian Chisnel, unknown, Carl Abraham, Dick Malone, unknown, Leola Warner, Jane Huhn.

1943 Smithfield High School "V" for victory: "Flicker", Peggy, Ruth, Roy, Bertha, "Defie", and Dorothy.

Smithfield School 1943 basketball team.

Smithfield School, 1930. The teacher in the center back row is Unk Abraham. First row, left to right: Elaine Cramer Gant, Betty Jane Preece, Mary Ray, Bonnie McCoy, Mabel McLaughlin, Imogene Hague, Alice Van Bremen, Winnie Fields. Second row: Bertha Mae Mayfield, Paul Britt, Virginia Everett, Charles Glunt, Marie McCann, Edward Moody, Anna Marie Wise, Paul Hastings, Olive Moore. Third row: Raymond Day, Ray Swanger, Anna Jane Kramer, Paul Romesburg, Florence Breakiron, Lester Robinson, ? Grant, Dorothy Downy, Tom Montieth. Fourth row: Rebecca Britt, Ruth Moser, Rose Field, Eva McDaniel, Fred Hartman, A. J. Stuck, Edna Reese, Elva Hardin, Robert Kisbaum. Fifth row: Charles Knight, Virginia Kirkwood, Frankie Wycott, Margaret Miller, and Virginia Miller.

Smithfield School, 1926 - teacher Mary Jenkins. Anna Jane Malone is the third girl from the right.

Weaver School, 1916 - teacher Minnie George. Students are playing "Ring-around-the-rosy".

The old Georges Creek Academy was built in 1856-1857, just outside Smithfield. It opened in 1857

Another view of the Georges Creek Academy.

The old Paul School in Ruble around 1910, with teacher Catherine Morgan. Seated, left to right: Guy Cooley, Harry Bowman, Glen Roderick, Harry Dils, Joseph Stewart, Ralph Collins, Jessie Roderick, George Williams, Raymond Doolittle, Robert Moser. Second row: Carl Roderick, Arthur Walls, John Williams, Jessie (Junior) Stewart, Walter Fowler, Joseph Moser, John Neverdale, Clyde Breakiron. Third row: Charles Sutton, Pearl Doolittle, Mary Conn, Maude Sutton, Mildred Doolittle, Retha Smith, Hazel Roderick, Pearl Breakiron, Lena Haneym, Brian Cooley, Harold Williams. Top row: Anna Williams, Abaline Doolittle, unknown, Bessie Bowman, Ida Fields.

The Tobin School House around 1920's. This was located between Route 857 and Woodbridge Hill.

Georges Township High School, 1935.

Glendale School, March 27, 1908 - This sat above Haydentown off Route 857.

Sheets Hill School, 1896. This was located between Point Marion and Smithfield on Route 119 near Morgan's Grove. First row, left to right: a Dusenberry, a Franks, Greg Rider, Harry R. Morgan, Oliver Morton, Ada Morton, Lulu Blosser, Edna Morgan, Carl Rider, Irene Corder, Addie Everly, Grace Flowers, a Dusenberry, Cora Frankenberry, Eva Blosser, a Blosser, a Blosser, Stewart Everly, George H. Morgan, Earl Morgan. Second row: Maude Rider, Laura Sackett, Caroline "Cad" Morgan, Kate Blosser, Archie West, Grace Warman, Teacher John Morris Hall, Lucy Morgan, Alice Frankenberry, Blanche Warman, a Blosser, Jesse Corder, Emily Morgan, Alverda Farr, Florence Riffle, Maria Morgan, Alice Molesy. Third row: Harry Morton, Owen Farr, William Morgan, Fred Warman, Daniel Morgan, Robert Sturgis, a Moats, Sturgis Frankenberry, Arthur Campbell, David Morgan, Robert Franks, LeRoy Campbell, Clyde Corder, Howard Morgan, Wade Riffle, Lindsay Franks, Benjamin Morgan, Lyons Morgan, unknown.

The Smithfield B & O Station with the Barton Hotel in the background. The men are standing in front of the fence which surrounds the pump. From left to right: Cal Black, Guy Dils, Charley Wise, Polly Huhn, Pedro Morgan, Charles Minard.

The old railroad station and tracks.

The deserted Smithfield B & O Station, June 1985.

The Smithfield B & O Roundhouse and shop was torn down in the late 1950's.

The big firebox, 1958.

The railroad tunnel at Outcrop around 1903.

Smithfield B & O Branch Crew and Yard Master, 1930. Left to right: E. I. Foye, C. H. Huhn, O. J. Feather, J. D. Grahm, O. Sutton, J. A. Matthews, J. D. Lowe.

The First Trick Shop Force, circa 1930. First row, left to right: T. Welch, F. G. Stuck, L. L. Robinson, D. C. McCoy, George May, E. Mayfield, James Capes, F. Ramsey, T. L. Hague, F. Grahm, John Capes. Second row: W. Brady, O. E. Carr, F. Moser, A. T. Powell, J. A. McDermott, R. Costella. Third row: A. Nester, L. Wilson, W. H. Bitner, G. Glover, H. W. Glover, H. B. Sheetz. Fourth row: C. S. Clemmer, T. S. Boyd, O. A. Morris.

1938 Smithfield rail yard.

Smithfield B & O Shop around 1950-52. Left to right: Ray Clawson, Happy Glover, J. A. McDermott, Harry Bitner, William Jordan, "Ducky" Clemmer, John Janosik, Jr., "Speed" Robinson on engine, John J. Smith, Harry McLaughlin, William Harbaugh, Charles Black, a Snain, Emmons Monaghan, Art Powell, and Cinder the dog.

An unknown miner from the Smithfield area.

Mike Rosinsky at the beehive ovens.

Repairing a beehive oven in the Smithfield area. This unknown man worked for Mart Adams.

Welder repairing tracks used to haul the coke.

Steve Shamrock in shovel.

Bowood Mine #2 with Joby Stuck, mine superintendent.

Leckrone strip with 300 Marion Shovel. Fred Malone, engineer and August Shiffbauer, crane operator. Circa 1936.

Leckrone strip, 1936.

The old Mary Ann Furnace on the George Cooley property, Haydentown.

Barton Hotel, 1912. Dora Breakiron, age 20, (standing on porch) was a cook and waitress here.

This was the old Campbell Hotel in the early 1800's. Photo take circa 1940 shows the Odd Fellows Hall, Bowman Hardware, the old hotel, and Perie Abraham's Antique Shop. John and Bernadine Smith and Mr. and Mrs. Tom Murray on steps.

The old Campbell Hotel sat across from today's Nicosia's Store. Photo taken in 1950. From left to right, first row: a Huntley boy, Bob Huntley, Evelyn Rowan, a Huntley girl, Becky Huntley, Frances Huntley, Ginger? Huntley. Second row: John Smith, Bill Jordan, Dolores Jordan, Vietta Noakes, Lela Jordan, Ila Rowan, Roberta Huntley, a Huntley girl, Bernadine Rowan.

Ed and Emma Conn's house at Woodbridgetown. In the windows are Saul Johnson and Lydia Miller Johnson. Third man from left is George Miller, then Elizabeth Miller. James Conn in beard by window. Margaret Conn next to him (child between them unknown).

C.A. Grannell residence (now 10 Church Street). Left to right: Bess Grannell, Neil Brown, a DeForest, Arthur Grannell, Ruth Grannell, unknown, Harry Grannell, and Mrs. Grannell.

The J. W. Weaver home around 1900.

Mary Moser Swaney doing her chores, 1918.

The Frankenberry Farm of Smithfield, Route 119 south.

1926 - Charles Breakiron on a Minneapolis Molene tractor with spike iron wheels on a Sleepy Hollow Farm.

The home of William James Breakiron, 1908. From left to right are daughters Hattie Wilson and Stella Colley, granddaughter Sadie Wilson, wife Sarah Jane Huey Breakiron, daughter Daisy L. Breakiron, son in arms is William Breakiron. William J. Breakiron is in the buggy with James Freeman McCormick on the extreme right. Leo Wilson is standing between the horses. The horses are Tom, John, Fanny and Byrd. "Bill" delivered milk and ice to Smithfield. He cut the ice from the creek below the house in the winter and packed it in sawdust in an ice shed for summer use.

John and Mollie Breakiron gathering hay in 1919 on a farm near Paull School with a three-horse team.

1985 aerial view of Smithfield.

Seghi's Five Lakes, Inc. of Rubles Mill, taken by Tom's Aerial Photos of Morgantown, WV. These are a group of regulated fishing "pay lakes" located 2 miles southeast of Smithfield. They are stocked with trout, catfish, bass, carp, etc. The first two lakes were opened in 1950 and built by Joe French. By 1961, the Seghi's, who had leased the lakes in 1956 and bought them the following year, built three more lakes.

A snow scene circa 1904, at the Rubles Mill Bridge.

The Phillip and Cynthia Rhodes family, circa 1902. First row, left to right: Joe, Katie, Maggie, Phillip, Frank, Cynthia, Charles (on lap), and Etta. Back row: Harry, Bessie, Billy, Sarah Jane. Photo taken at the old Rhodes home place in Hardin Hollow. About a year after this photo, Cynthia died. Later, Phillip married Ella Braddee and had 17 more children with a grand total of 29.

Otis Cooley, Homer Cooley, Guy Saylor, Lloyd Fowler, and Junior Stewart, 1918.

A quilting bee in 1905 on Liberty Street (now Jack Fritz's place).

The Women's Christian Temperance Union, circa 1900. Front row, left to right: Mary Miller, Mary Thomas, Perie Abraham, Daisy Frankenberry Jackson, "Kate" Campbell Brooks, Nellie Hays. Back row: Etta Hays, Mabel Sutton, Ethel Sutton, Mrs. Curtain Show, Lewis Hastings, Alice Ramsey, Mollie Abraham.

August 8. 1904 - a group at Alex Brownfield's place on Glendale School Road.

1909 group at White Rocks. Left to right: Fred Huhn, Ethel Adams, Jesse Ryan, Marie Goforth, Don Abraham, Ethel Sutton.

1909 group at White Rocks. Left to right: Ethel Sutton, Grannell Whetzell, Marie Goforth, Anna Dunn.

1909 group at White Rocks, front, left to right: Ernest Granger, Nell Britt. Second row: Jess Ryan, Sara Abraham, Anna Dunn, Nell Whetzell, Ira Ryan, Marie Goforth. Third row: Stella Lowe, Don Abraham, Belle Pollock, Daisy Frankeyberry, Ethel Sutton, Fred Huhn.

C. J. Crannell and C. D. Crow, circa 1900.

The John Riffle residence between Smithfield and Morris Crossroads. Left to right: Nicholas, Wade, John Quincy, Florence, Edna, and Martha Bixler Riffle.

Picnicking at White Rocks.

The B. S. Conn residence, September 14, 1901. Left to right: Della Miller Conn, Bessie, Benjamin Stewart, Arthur, and Marie Conn. The residence was located on Haydentown Road.

Photo taken at the Monaghan Farm betweeen 1898-1900. Left to right: Florence, Grarrett, Walter, Emmons, and Anna Sturgis Monaghan.

Mutt Moser in front of the Bank Building.

Smithfield Rotary Club, 1985. First row, left to right: Wayne Reese, Jim Terry, Sam Sheehan, Dan Chess, Jim Vance, Jim ? Second row: George Cooley, Eveny, Bob Maukutsa, Amadee Merbedone, John Weller, Myron Warman, Chuck Cylinski.

1946 York Run Grange Group, Standing, left to right: Kate Jones, Ethel Grannell, Ida Conn, Clara Horton, Mabel Wise, Walter Kiger. Kneeling: Alice Morton Fox, Dora Brown, Mrs. James Kingan, Kathryn Fields Kiger, unknown.

Ida Rowan in her 1932 Chevrolet. Keifel house shown.

Henry Deffenbaugh had a farm near Old Frame.

Donald McCann after his return from France and World War I.

John and Nancy Davis. John was Deacon and Trustee at the Mt. Moriah Church, 1870.

Smithfield holiday parade.

Smithfield's first fire truck.

Mr. and Mrs. A. A. Moser's Wedding day at Rubles Mill, 190?. Left to right: James Miller, Mary Ramsey Miller, Andy and Marie Moser.

A 1906 picnic at Rubles Mill.

The James Miller residence at Rubles Mill - the corner of Ruble and Haydentown Road.

The Jones house on Woodbridge Road, 1902. Left to right: Lavina Jones Swaney, Dora Jones Ruble, Perie Swaney, and Frances Jones Bryte.

A. F. Hill, author of the White Rocks or The Robber's Den - A Tragedy in the Mountains, published by Acme Press of Morgantown, WV in 1900.

Sarah Jane Davis Jones, wife of Jesse Evans Jones, mid 1860's.

Jesse Evans Jones, Civil War Veteran, mid 1860's.

Jerry Jones, son of James and Anna Ross Jones, died at Salisbury, NC Civil War prison.

A mock lynching at Rubles Mill.

A cyclone hits Smithfield in 1905. Left to right: Mary Jackson, Mrs. Reed, Gene Reed, Mr. Reed, Lon Divel, George Campbell.

Paul School after the tornado of June 23, 1944.

The Ruble Dam and Falls that ran the mill. This is above the bridge, 1903-05.

Yesteryear In Point Marion

Point Marion is situated in the extreme southern tip of Fayette County, where the Cheat and Monongahela Rivers come together. The elevation is 812 feet.

The following are dates and historic happenings of the small river town:

1770 - The site of Point Marion Borough was patented to John Wilson. It was known at this time as Gist's Point.

1780-1839 - There were about 350 slaves registered in Fayette County. At this time, Point Marion was known as Gist's Point, where both Dr. James Ramsey and the Honorable Theopholis Phillips had slaves.

1789 - There were two saw mills and three grist mills in operation in Springhill Township.

1789 - (At least) 22 stills were producing a total daily yield of 1202 gallons of whiskey each day in Springhill Township.

1801 - John Sadler purchased the land from John Wilson which later became the borough of Point Marion.

March, 1817 - The General Assembly passed a new law which allowed stock companies to build and operate lock and dam systems to be maintained by tolls.

March 15, 1842 - John Sadler, grandson of John Sadler (above), laid out the town of Point Marion. This consisted of three streets: Cheat, Water and High. Each street was fifty feet wide. He sold lots at a public sale this day. The person who bought the first lot received the honor of naming the town. Seth Stafford purchased Lot #1, which was located on the point, for $100.00. He named the town in honor of General Frances Marion, better known as the "Swamp Fox" of the Revolutionary War. Many local soldiers had served under the General and a book *The Life of General Francis Marion* was quite popular at this time. Lots number 2 and 3 were bought by Robert Beatty.

1843 - Seth Stafford had the first house built in Point Marion. A black man named Samuel Patterson constructed it.

The first doctor was Dr. Oglevee.

The first merchant was Hudson Higinbotham.

The first Burgess (Chief administrative officer of an unincorporated borough) was Jacob Conn.

1856 - Six locks had been completed to New Geneva.

1862 - The Methodist Episcopal Church was built.

1863 - Jacob Ruble had a Cooper's Shop on Cheat Street. Simeon McClain, Absolam McClain, Andrew Gallatin, and James Board worked there.

1867 - Ira Keyser, Ambrose Dillinger, Bowen Crow, and A. D. Frankenberry built a saw mill on the point between the two rivers. In 1889 Crow and Dillinger dropped out of the business, but the mill prospered for at least half a century.

1867 - Point Marion had 11 houses, one store, and a Methodist Church. Mail was delivered each Saturday from New Geneva, the closest Post Office.

1871 - John A. Clark built his first (of five) saw mills. It sat at the head of Hope Hollow and was destroyed by a flood soon after its construction.

1872 - Clark and Dillinger built a saw mill at Crow's Ferry.

1874 - Clark built a saw mill and a planning mill close to where the Cheat River Bridge's south end sits. After a cyclone badly damaged them, he rebuilt and ran the business until 1888. In 1888, a flood tore the structures from their foundations and wrecked his equipment. In 1889, he built a mill on Freeling Street.

1880 - Point Marion got its first post office. It was in Morris and Keiser's store at Penn and Main Streets. Sam Morris became postmaster and Absolam McClain, Jr. took on the route of carrying the mail three times a week to and from New Geneva. For this he was paid 25 cents per round trip. He normally carried 10 letters and 4 papers. In 1883, the government established a mail carrying route between Point Marion, Smithfield, and Morgantown, WV.

1882 - Huling and Company built a large saw mill at Crow's Ferry which was destroyed by the flood of 1888.

1883 - Lock #7 was constructed.

1886 - W. J. Ruble and T. J. Keiser built a grist mill in Point Marion. They ran it until 1900 and sold it to W. L. South.

1887 - The Dewing Lumber Mill went into operation, sawing millions of lumber feet per year. Logs were brought in down the Cheat River by transporting them on log rafts from Tucker and Randolph Counties in West Virginia. The land they purchased for the mill was owned by Michael and Ann Cagey (brother and sister). It sits on the east side of the Monongahela River about 1/2 mile from the Cheat's mouth. The mill's heavy equipment was shipped by rail to Pittsburgh, then transferred to four barges and taken to Protzman's Landing. This was the head of the Slackwater. Lock #8 had not yet been completed. The lighter machinery was shipped to Point Marion on flatboats run by Norman H. Young, Abram DeGardeyn, Sr., August Nelson, and Abraham Williams. Heavier equipment was hauled by four horses and a yoke of oxen. The piers were built by Elmer Cagey and Isaac Blosser of hickory and oak. They filled each with 500 cubic yards of stone. The mill ran only six months a year because of log supply, but put out 40,000 feet per day. In 1890, they built a planning mill, shipping much of their product to a company they owned in Kalamazoo, Michigan. At noon on June 6, 1899, the last of the boards were sawed. The saw mill was dismantled and shipped on the railway a year later. The planning mill was moved to Nilan, Pennsylvania, where they converted it into a saw mill.

1887 - M. A. Campbell's Spoke Factory, and E. D. Bierer's Sash and Door Factory were operating here.

1888 - The disciple Church was erected.

1890 - J. C. and Simeon McClain began the McClain Brothers Sand Company. Until 1946, sand and gravel were big business here.

September 11, 1893 - Point Marion was incorporated into a borough with 103 acres of land and 450 residents.

1893 - The borough's public school originated with 105 pupils and Professor A. J. Gans.

1894 - The F. M. and P. branch of the B & O Railroad was completed, bringing the first passenger train here.

1895 - The Guffey and Queen gas belt of Springhill Township was developed. They had three flowing wells 1600, 1800 and 3200 feet deep in Greene County, and one well in the borough of Point Marion 1400 feet deep.

1899 - A flouring mill was built by Keyser, Holbert, and Company. This was run by L. M. Cooper.

1899 - William L. Stewart was Burgess.

1899 - The following were Point Marion merchants: W. L. Stewart, S. G. Smith, A.L. Stone, T.J. Keyser, E.P. Durr, J.N. Conn, C.H. Schriser, and Mac Newcomer.

1899 - During this time of development potter's clay was taken from Eberhart Farm and used in new Geneva potteries. Fruit and berry culture was also "blossoming"

1899 - Town doctors were Dr. L. N. Burchinal and S. B. Owen.

1899 - Andrew Haas managed a hotel.

1899 - The Methodist Protestant Church was built.

1900 - The Morris Glass Company was built by Morris, Lemley, and Wildman. This manufactured bottles.

June 9, 1900 - The Jeannette Glass Company, Ltd., was formed in Point Marion. By 1902, their production was up to more than a (railway) car load per day.

1902 - The First National Bank opened.

November 4, 1902 - Federated Window Glass Company incorporated, with Leon J Houze, Sr. as President.

1911 - The L. J Houze Convex Glass Company was formed. It was incorporated in 1917 In 1923 both Federated and Portrait Window Glass Company merged with L. J. Houze Convex Glass Company.

1921 - The library was opened to the public.

The McClain Sand Company, circa 1930. The towboat is "Togo" This is the point where the Cheat and Monongahela Rivers come together, with Point Marion in the background.

The Jeannette Glass Company, 1909.

These are workmen at Houze Glass Factory, who are laying the foundation for a new building around 1920. William Stewart is on the right.

Dewing's Sawmill was built on the east side of the Monongahela, about a half mile from the mouth of the Cheat in 1887. They operated only six months out of the year, but put out 40,000 feet of lumber per day. From left are: third man in second row wearing hat is Abe DeGardeyn, Sr., sixth man in second row holding straw hat is Abe DeGardeyn, Jr., third man in third row with black hair is Isaac DeGardeyn, and the fourth man in the last row wearing strap overalls is John DeGardeyn, Sr.

This strip mine was on Locust Hill near Fallen Timbers during World War I. This shovel was brought from the Panama Canal!

James D. Clark owned Clark's Lumber Mill in Point Marion and was a well respected businessman. 1884-1979.

May 1940 - coal tipple on Ira Burchinal's farm in Fallen Timbers.

Harry Crawford, May 4, 1913 with beehive coke ovens in the background.

This mill was located near New Geneva.

1905-1906 near Dewing Mill. This house was being moved from the river bottom to the top of the hill. James Baker third from left.

The old B & O Station, turn of the century.

A crowd at the B & O Station, before it burned in 1923.

Taking a Sunday stroll along the tracks near Cheat Haven. Left to right: Earl Deffenbaugh, Julie Baker, Lola Deffenbaugh, Ira Fast, Marge Baker, Gurnie Baker, Playford Sisler.

Coal train going through Point Marion around 1920.

Frank Baker and team working a team near Morris Crossroads.

The men here are farming a plot which is now Freeling Street. Quinter Stewart is on the left, holding the reigns. Clark's Saw Mill on right. The Lewellan House is in the background. Colts in front of the team.

Penn Street at the railroad crossing in 1933.

Penn Street at the railroad crossing in 1960.

Depositing a letter in front of the post office in 1942.

Looking down Penn Street, with Dora Lockard Livery on left and Brunswick Pool & Billiards on right. Circa 1900.

Ross Brother's Grocery on right. Sipe's Lunch on left, 1960.

Frank Stewart's place in the late 1920's.

Another view of Frank Stewart's place in the late 1920's.

John Wildey's Blacksmith Shop in back of Sadler Street, early 1900's.

Aerial view of Point Marion, 1910.

Aerial view of Point Marion, 1946.

L. J. Houze Convex Glass Company, 1946.

"The Point", where the Cheat and Monongahela Rivers unite, 1946.

An early photo of U. S. Lock #8 on the Monongahela River.

A 1915 view of the Cheat River's Selser Rock.

A relaxing day canoeing at Inspiration Point.

The steamer "Wabash" around 1900, made trips between Morgantown and Brownsville. Captain William H. Lloyd is in the vest to the right.

This barge was called the "Ted B" and belonged to the McClain Sand Company, circa 1930.

Docked at the Landing is the L. C. Woodward from Fairmont, West Virginia.

Keener Stewart used this skiff to cross the river from his home on the Greene County side to his place of work at the Houze Glass Factory.

Left to right are Jake Blosser, John Clark, and Keener Stewart, after a day of hauling logs on a wooden raft to a lumber mill.

The County Bridge over the Cheat River at the turn of the century.

The Albert Gallatin Bridge over the Monongahela was completed in 1930 to connect Point Marion with Greene County.

This is the Cheat River Bridge before the Lake Lynn Dam. Pictured standing in an area that is now under water are John, Kathryn, Hagan, Dora, unknown, and Charles Gates, July 4, 1911.

New Geneva Pottery being hauled by A. Mackinson, F. Neal, and L. Rumble on a Pottery Ark or Broad-Horn Boat.

A 1916 photo of the Central Hotel with what appears to be the staff posing for this postcard.

The Colonial Hotel is having an addition constructed in this photo, circa 1907

The Colonial Hotel showing new addition in 1917

The Springhill Cottage, with the Monongahela River in the background, was a summer resort for Pittsburgh folks.

The Castle Keiser was built in the early 1900's at Nilan as a Cheat River summer resort.

Camp Run Skating Rink in 1919.

This was the home of James and Laura Baker on Blasser Hill, about one mile north of Point Marion, circa 1900.

The Thomas Ramsey Home was built in 1780 near Mt. Moriah Church, on the road between Fallen Timbers and New Geneva. The original land grant is dated 1773.

Relaxing on the porch of the Osborne Hare home from left to right are: Nancy Hare, Chancey Conn, Plessie Hare, and Elizie Durr, circa 1900. Elzie had stores in Point Marion and Cheat Haven. This house burnt in 1939. The John Goff House is now at this location.

The R. R. Robinson home under construction by contractors Ira Burchinal and Enlow Lockard. Robert H. Ross is standing. Robert Ross Robertson and his bride, Carrie, are in the carriage.

The Trinity Methodist Church after it was remodeled. This is a church membership group from 1940.

The Trinity Methodist Church was built in 1900 on Sadler Street.

Trinity Methodist Church Youth Group, 1930.

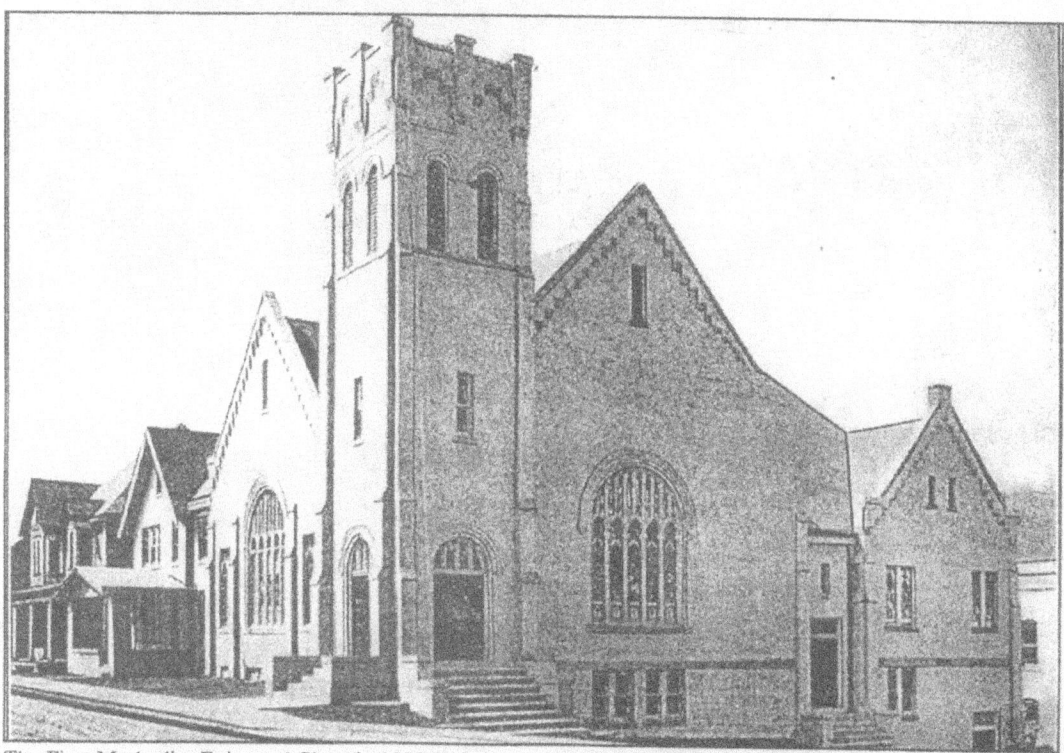
The First Methodist Episcopal Church, 1926. This is now the United Methodist Church.

The St. John's Lutheran Church is also known as the L. C. or Brick Church. Photo circa 1900.

The Trinity Lutheran Church in Cheat Haven, 1900.
This is now called the Lake Lynn Chapel.

The Point Marion High School, circa 1930.

Point Marion "Public School" opened in 1893 with 105 pupils and Professor A. J. Gans. Photo circa 1912.

J. Earl Roberts and Sam Jacobs were two respected educators in Point Marion from the 1920's to the 1940's. Under their leadership, Point Marion High School became one of the finest schools in the state.

The Point Marion Board of Education, 1942. Left to right: Dr. A. D. Hunger, Houston Board, Frank L. Bowers, Joseph Siegel, and Dr. Gilbert Bertiaux.

The Point Marion Elementary School around 1900. This photo was taken at Ben Berg's Store on Penn Street. Ernie Conn Lyons was the teacher. Front row, fifth from left is Bertie Miller; seventh from left is Ruth McClain. Back row, second from right is Stella Stewart; third from right is Becky Stewart (small girl).

Point Marion School group with A. J. Gans, teacher. Circa 1907-10.

Point Marion High School Junior Varsity Basketball Team, 1916. First row, left to right: Theron Provona, Frank Ross, Artrhur Hoard, Albert La Poe. Second row: Raymond McClain, Assistant Principal and Team Manager, Charles Stewart, Harry Berg, Stanley P. Miller, and Milo Ruse.

Graduating Class of 1917, Point Marion High School. First row, left to right: Arthur Hoard, Elmer Van Zandt, Elizabeth Blosser, unknown, Helen Hildebrand, John Blosser, unknown, Theron Provance, Evelyn Berg, Milo Ruse, Frank Ross, and Raymond McClain. Second row: Earl Fowler, Mildred Hildebrand, Stanley Miller, Marie Everly, Harry Berg, Marquerite Wildey, Charles Stewart, Marie Priester, and Albert LaPoe.

Point Marion First Grade Class, 1917, with teacher Stella Frankenberry. Ephriam C. Tyler is in the back row, seventh from the left.

Point Marion High School Class of 1917 putting on a "Spirit of '76" Pageant. Left to right: George Phillips, Cecil Conn, unknown, Kemp Conn, Raoul Frere and Herman Young.

The Fallen Timbers School before it was moved across the road due to a strip mine. Photo taken before WWI.

Fallen Timbers School, 1901. Front row, left to right: Harry Clemmer, Ray Day, Jordan Crow, Frank Crow, Howard Crow, Thomas Moser, James Moser, Thomas Board, Charles Board, Virgil Clemmer, Millie Sackett Robinson, Nellie Board Stewart, Frances "Fanny" Crow Leib, Maudy Moser, Mabel Hall, Elizabeth Black, Leotta Crow Stoner, Lola Crow Heart, Tillie Moser, Sarah Day Hixenbaugh. Second row: Lillie Crow, Rachel Styson, Stella Stevenson, Marie Marie Styson, Millie Caseber Cagey, Lucy Cagey Clark, Virgil Beardsley, Ella Clemmer, Earnest Birch, Cameron Burchinal, Frank Board, George Frankenberry, Jess Frankenberry, Finley Moser, Arbeth Black, Doswan Black, Pearl Crow, Lizzie Moser Smith, Clara Board, Lucy Board Evans, Pierie Cagey Crow, Emma Board Evans. Third row: Jerry Crow, Emma Clemmer Boyer, William Moser, Walter Rhodes, Hubert Stoner, Teacher John Hall, Martin Stoner, Fred Frankenberry, Bertha Black Conn, Anna Burchinal Baker, Millie Stoner, Rhodes. Top: Mabel Rhodes, unknown.

Marion School, 1926. The Marion School was located on Blasser Hill, one mile north of Point Marion and housed grades one through eight. First row, left to right: Gene Klink, Quinter Baker, Jess Colebank, Stanley Diel, Irving Dils, Theodore Klink, James Baker. Second row: Jane Ball, Dorothy Board, Mary Board, Margaret Crow, Marvin Dils, Cecil Crow, William Colebank, Noel Ball, Laurie Ball. Third row: Lawrence Stemmlar, Art Hershman, Paul Lewis, Stanley Dils, Raymond Goff, Thelma Dils, Edith Crow. Fourth row: Donald Crow, Clarence Stewart, Virginia Colebank, Clara Stemmler. Fifth row: Mrs. Carlier, Hugh Lewis, Carl Crow, Ila Dils, Nellie Brown.

Fallen Timbers School, 1910-12, Greg Rider, teacher. Pictured left to right are: Annie Frankenberry, Rosalynn Hall, Helen Hall, Elizabeth Provance, unknown, ? Vanderness, ? Caseber, Earl Lynn, Harry Williams, Hazel Crow, Madonna Evans, Leora Provance, Wynona Lackey, unknown, Irene Provance, Lou Hazel Moser, unknown, Lenora Lynn, Charles Keiser, Howard Evans, George Moser, Tommy Evans, Howard Crow, Millie Sackett, Louis Caseber, Wade Grimes, Minor Provance, Edward Crow, Rhetta Board, James Moser, Donald Evans, Willard Keiser, Ira Keiser, Ruth Rhodes, Fannie Crow, Bessie Grimes, Asia Crow, Grey Rider, teacher; and Idella Touch.

Fallen Timbers Grade School, 1932-33. Bottom row, left to right: Belle Wertz Crow, William Billy Jennings, Beatrice Clemmer Reed, Lewis Junior Caseber, Elaine Bruni Gatto, Ruth Wertz Stewart, Bernard Murray, Richard Griffin. Second row: Armand Bruni, Jane Ball Clemmer, Noel Ball, Mrs. Bertha Franks, teacher, Rudolph Bruni, Genevieve Clemmer Dunham, Mildred Jennings Cage, Spenser Clemmer. Third row: Charles Junior Griffin, Chester Clemmer, Joseph Kubala, Theodore Ted Kubala, Lillian Caseber, Charles Boyer, Lena Caseber Carlier, Peggy Pruitt Proden. Top row: Donald Murray, Lillian Warman Reed, Lowry Ball, Louise Griffin Blosser, James Jim Clark, Edward Kubala, George Clemmer, Stella Kubala Bertovich.

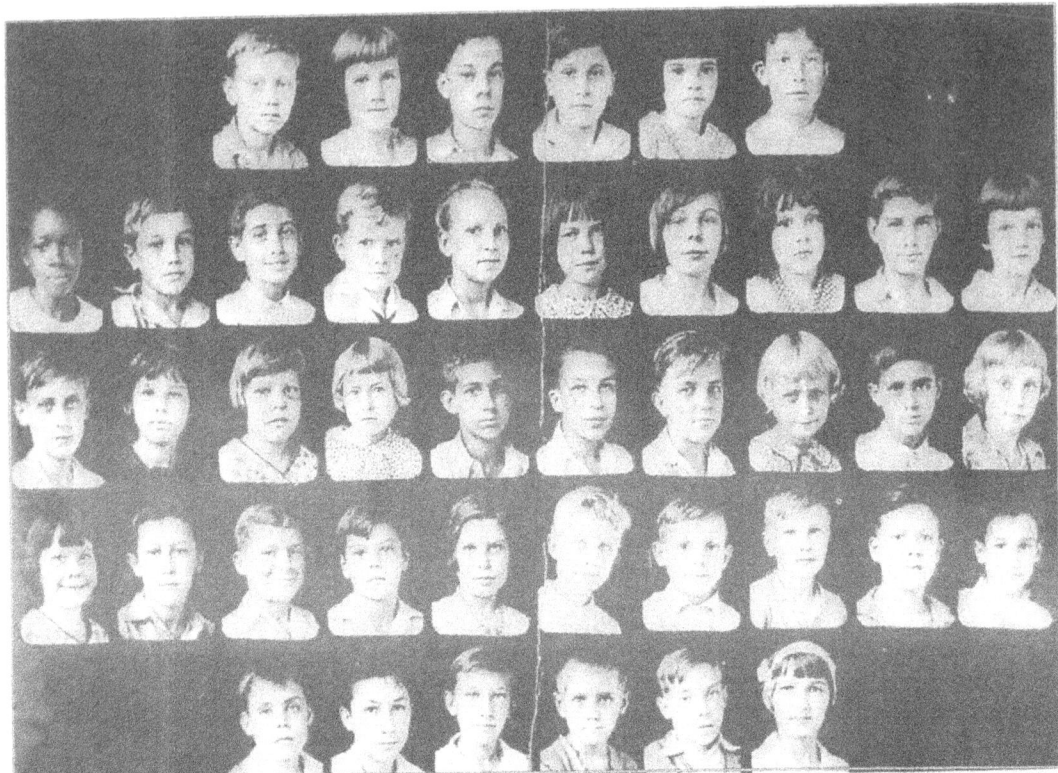

Marion School, 1930. Top row, left to right: Derwood Diwitt, Helen Jane Sisley, Paul Lewis, Duane Smouse, Betty Ganoe, Hoffa Sullivan, Second row: Virginia Robison, Jess Colebank, Marvin Dils, Laird Sisley, Art Hershman, Dorothy Board, Mary Board, Betty Roads, Irving Dils, Daisy Ganoe. Third row: Theodore Klink, Helen Sullivan, Edith Board, Margaret Helen Hostetler, Stanley Dils, Lawrence Stemmlar, Cecil Crow, Thursda Hostetler, Bob Dils, Florence Klink. Fourth row: Elizabeth Board, Quinter Baker, Jim Sisley, I. N. Glover, Cathy Glover, Elwood Diel, Cecil Hershman, Bill Colebank, Rayond Goff, Charles Baker Fifth row: Andy Glover, Jim Baker, Stanley Diel, Kenny Dils, Gene Klink, Margaret Crow.

Friendship Hill School, 1898, with teacher William Conn.

Friendship Hill School, 1898, with teacher Miss Robinson.

Cheat Hill or Conn School on Stewartstown Road, 1906. Left to right, top row: Delph Titus, Lloyd Fowler, Luther Ross, Raymond Conn, Mary Schroyer, Cora Sargent, Betty Shallenberger, W.G. Conn, Principal. Middle row: Alice Cabaret, Rita Quineff, Catherine Raymond, Artie Miller, Ethel Schroyer Hunter, Pete Raymond. Bottom row: Margarite Raymond, Margarete Condon, Sara Schroyer, Bertie Miller, Blanche Fowler, Alfred Statsen, Jules Quineff, Earle Fowler.

York Run School, 1911.

Filbert Public School, 1916. Gertrude Crawford is in the back row, fifth from the left.

Gans Hill School class of 1909-10. Front row, left to right: Willis Hall, John High, Cameron Snyder, Lewis Gans, Willis Dils, Howard Evans, Nellie Heath, Laishley Blosser, Ina Brink, Anna Swope, Berth Black, teacher. Center: Howard Crow, Herman Blosser, Grace Blosser, Louisa Ramsey, Senith High, Oran Hall, Clarence Robinson, Charles Robinson, Lonnie Crow, Janet Hall, Anna High, Harry Robinson, Nellie Drew, Marie Heath. Top: Blanche Campbell, Lillian Drew, Mildred Gans, Bessie Drew, Pauline Heath, and Elizabeth Blosser.

Belgian Relief Committee, July 14, 1915. This is one of four parts of a panoramic photograph taken at Camp Run Park.

Friendship Hill Estate workers, 1910. These Point Marion men were restoring the mansion.

Bill Moser was Chief of Police in Point Marion for 40 years, until his retirement in 1964.

John and Josephine Goff owned a dairy on Blosser Hill in the 1930's and 40's. Charles Baker, Jr., is shown sitting on their truck, circa 1940.

These Point Marion men are on a fishing trip in Canada. Left to right are: Cal Roher, Jack Thomas, Cecil Sutton, Jack Foltz, Sylvester Stillwagon, Cecil Conn, Kemp Conn, Ralph Simpkins.

This group of men were possibly working on the roads. Lloyd Colebank is in the lower left corner. Left to right: Ernest Conn, Charlie Newcomer, Jess Costello, John McClain, Leonard Sidwell, Bill Stewart, Arthur Lucas, engineer; and Ed Lapae.

The Point Marion Boy Scout Troop, circa 1925. Lloyd Stewart was Scoutmaster and took this photo.

Early Point Marion baseball team, 1910. Front row, left to right: John McClain, Chas. Newcomer, Chauncy Dils, unknown, Jim Ruble. Back row: John Jones, 3 unknowns, and Lawrence Dils.

Front row, left to right: Etta and Alice Crawford. Back row: Delia, Mary, and Pierson Crawford, Sade, Lida, and George Benjamin Liston.

The funeral of Samuel Hager, who died in the first World War. The American Legion is named after him. Lloyd Stewart is the lead Boy Scout in the procession.

Ann C. Hall was the granddaughter of Absolomon Morris, Morris Crossroads' founder. Seated, left to right: Ann C. Morris Hall, Emma Alice hall Burchinal. Standing: Carrie Hall Gans, Lizzie Hall Burchinal.

James and Phoebe (Pierson) Crawford, 1870.

These are the children and spouses of Daniel and Rebecca Stewart at an August 14, 1909 (1st Stewart) reunion. First row, left to right: Jesse and Myrtle Blosser, Jerry and Belle Stewart, and Bill and Sis Johnson. Second row: Quinter and Eva Stewart, David and Anna Stewart, and Jack and Elizabeth Stewart. Back row: William and Sara Stewart and Clark and Pet Sap.

The Deffenbaugh family lived on a farm between Smithfield and Old Frame. Left to right: Salina, Earl Nellie, Lola, Emma and Sylvanus Deffenbaugh. Salina and Sylvanus were twins.

This is the funeral of Seneth Robson Stewart, March 16, 1909, at the old Point Marion Cemebert. Left to right: Mrs. John (Anna) Crow, Jesse Stewart, Mack and Audrey Stewart, Ann Hall, Sally Stewart, Plessie Hare, unknown, Grandma Stewart, Elz Frankenberry, ? Stewart, Belle, George, Sara, Bessie, Harry and William Stewart, George Ogden, Mandy Neighbors, Ella Ogden, Ollie Stewart.

The children of Alice and Lloyd Colebank. Left to right: Virginia, William, Jesse and Elizabeth.

Gordon Baker, a major contributor to this book, in 1943 in his Red Ryder cowboy suit.

The Moser family posing on the front porch in 1924. Seated, left to right: David, Herbert, Irene, Bernice (on Irene's lap), Charles, Phyllis, (on Charles' lap), Margaret and Rupert (boy in front of post) Moser. Ada Carr Hood, Jimmie Hood, Earl Carr, Andrew and Mabel (on Andrew's lap) McCann, Mae Moser McCann Ramsey, Ruben McCann (on Mae's lap), Anna Frances and Marie McCann. Charles Moser is seated on ground. Grandma Kathryn Moser is seated on a chair on the porch. Standing: Gertrude, Will, Ila (with dog), and Martha Moser, William Swaney (in Martha's arms), Mary Moser Swaney (in back), Effie Moser, Elza Swaney (man in back), Walter Moser (by porch post), Kathryn "Kitty" George, Minnie Moser George (Weaver School teacher), Anna and Oren Carr, Lydia, Abraham, Stella, and Harry Moser.

Raymond Goff on a plane that was built by the Baker Boys of Blosser Hill in 1927, as a replica of the "Spirit of St. Louis" This is the same year Lindberg flew over the Atlantic. Goff is flying it in tire swing after the plane was wrecked and lost its nose and tail. Plane built by Osborne James, and Quinter and Charles Baker. It served as a landmark along Route 119 north of Point Marion for many years.

Rena and Ruth Stewart, Bill Cline, Charlie and Lloyd Stewart after the hunt, 1910.

Sunday afternoon on the Baker's front porch near Cheat Haven. Left to right: Jesse Baker, Milton McCormick, Joe and Bess Baker, Joe and Bess McCormick, Jerry and Lizzie Burchinal, Gurnie, Marge, Grove, Burchinal (baby), and Annie Baker.

George Baker of Cheat Haven about 1860.

Margaret Baker, wife of George, of Cheat Haven, 1860.

Ruth and Rena are the twin daughters of Sara and William Stewart who caused a sensation when they were born in 1905.

The Jerry Stewart Family. Left to right: Ed, Jerry, Lizzie, Sara and Jessie. In 1897, very shortly after this was taken, Lizzie and Sara were killed by a fire in their Point Marion home.

Audrey Blosser married Lloyd "Shock" Stewart. She was the daughter of Charles and Belle Blosser and posed for this photo here with her two best buddies.

These are the children of John and Mary Nieman, circa 1900. Left to right: Norma, Lula, and Jessie. Jessie taught school in Point Marion for 50 years.

These are believed to be the first members of Point Marion's American Legion.

Fred and Cameron Burchinal were cousins who lived at Fallen Timbers.

Coon hunting pals Henry Curg Lycurgus Rhoads and Will Stewart pose in front of the Stewart home on Sadler Street after a successful hunt. The dog on the right was "Quill" who howled his head off when the local church bells rang.

Books by Marci McGuinness

How to be a Working Author/Writer (2005; 2nd Edition, Fall 2008)
Chesapeake Bay Blue Crabs (2004)
In it to Win It (2001)
The Explorer's Guide to the Youghiogheny River, Ohiopyle and SW PA Villages (2000)
Along the Baltimore & Ohio Railroad, from Cumberland to Uniontown (1998)
Stone House Legends & Lore (1998)
Yesteryear at the Uniontown Speedway (1996)
Official Program U.S.A. Speedway, 1916 Reprint (1996)
Yesteryear in Ohiopyle - The Movie
Yesteryear in Smithfield (1996)
Yesteryear in Masontown (1994)
Yesteryear in Ohiopyle and Surrounding Communities, Volume III (2008)
Yesteryear in Ohiopyle and Surrounding Communities, Volume II (1994)
Yesteryear in Ohiopyle and Surrounding Communities, Volume I (1993)

Marci McGuinness is a southwestern Pennsylvania native. Her loves of Ohiopyle and the written word have led her to record local history, so that it is not lost in the "progress shuffle."

The author has written and published over 20 regional books and magazines since 1981. She also served as Marketing Director, then, Managing Editor, at the prestigious Cornell Maritime Press/Tidewater Publishers in Centreville, Maryland. There she published books by dozens of authors and professors on Chesapeake Bay and Maritime topics.

Today, McGuinness resides in Chalk Hill, Pennsylvania with her Jack Russell Terrier, Jake. She is presently launching reprints of all of her *Yesteryear* books in addition to the new title, *Yesteryear in Ohiopyle*, Volume III.

Under production for 2009 release are: *Gone to Ohiopyle, Haunted Laurel Highlands, Yesteryear in Ohiopyle, Volume IV* and *Murder in Ohiopyle and Other Tales.*

Visit her at ohiopyle.info or shorepublications.info.
Contact her at:
shorepublications@yahoo.com.